ISBN 978 0 86071 745 4

A Commissioned Publication Printed by

MOORLEYS
Print, Design & Publishing
info@moorleys.co.uk · www.moorleys.co.uk

To the memory of my Mum and Dad and to my family with my love and gratitude.

Acknowledgements

I shall forever he grateful to my family for their unfailing support, dedication and patience in putting this book together. Also to the people who provided the subject matter, some knowingly and others who, as total strangers to me had no idea that their simple acts or comments would appear in a book of verse. My unreserved thanks to Patrick, Ann and Tracey at Moorleys Print & Publishing for their advice, their patient understanding and for always being available. Nothing was ever too much trouble. And finally a special thank you to Leanne Scoins for allowing me to use her wonderful appraisal of my first book as the Foreword for this one. I am indebted to you all.

K.R. Warner

Foreword

Dear Mr Warner

Thank you for encouraging me to read the poems in your book 'Observations and Interpretations', you should be very proud, I enjoyed them very much. They have a clear style and personal identity and are very well observed. I liked your strong use of everyday language and themes, which I believe gives your work a wide appeal and reach. There is a real, tangible sadness as you explore personal and parental regret, ageing and fear of death. This you couple well with wit and humour and your description of love; at times very touching. For example, 'Harmony'. The pieces I love the most were 'My Friend', 'Memory Lane', 'A Fruitless Life', 'See you Anon', 'Did I Peek at Paradise' and 'Ireland's Little Men'. Here the language and rhythm seem to flow particularly well, it felt as though your emotions controlled the words and were not constrained in any way by poetic convention, there was a particular freedom. Keep up the good work.

– Leanne Scoins, 29/9/2014

Preface

Rhymes of Life is an updated version of my previous book, 'Observations and Interpretations' published in 2013 in conjunction with New Generation Publishing and withdrawn from publication in June 2016. The updated version contains most of the original work plus 25 rhymes not included in its predecessor, although many were published in the Kindle version, now no longer available.

As in my earlier effort the rhymes are presented in chronological order, with most of the material drawn from observations of people going about their everyday lives, and are interpretations of their reactions to varying experiences, portrayed in the form of rhyme. Whilst others are simply the product of my imagination.

Contents

The Site Fixer

Site fixers are a worthy breed
Victims of employer's greed,
Missing wives and children small
This job could drive you up the wall,
Trying hard to make ends meet
Enough to keep us off the street.

The hours are long the money short
If only people gave a thought
To lonely nights in lonely bars
And supping almost endless jars
Of local bitter, G and T
Back and forwards for a pee.

Girls offer comfort at a price
Ah! Just another sacrifice
That we poor fixers have to make
Not for us the juicy steak,
But fish and chips out of a bag
And sharing them with some old slag.

With fine chalk line and trusty level
Scribing tools and sliding bevel
To work out cuts in awkward corners
Too difficult for bench hand joiners,
Who send things to the site left long
Marked - cut on site - it might be wrong.

Keeping the company name intact
It's down to us and that's a fact,
Working more but getting less
The fixer's life is just a mess,
Hoping for a better price
And even then, it won't suffice.

Grafting hard for next to 'nowt'
While the gaffers sit and gloat,
Wearing out their trouser seats
Yapping on the phone of feats
That they performed so long ago,
When they were on the tools you know.

King of the Fixers

He stands five feet eight and a little bit
This man whose mitres always fit,
He splices joints that can't be seen
And other men can only dream
Of emulating him someday,
Alas no matter how they pray
That day will never come to pass
No one will ever reach his class.

With nail bag firmly fixed in place
He sets to at a furious pace
Fixing shop fronts, frames and doors
You'll hardly ever see him pause,
From one job to the next he flies
Mere mortals can't believe their eyes,
The job is done, it's two weeks early,
The boss man rubs his hands and fairly
Bounces up and down with glee
Crying that's an extra grand for me.

His colleagues stand and stare in wonder
It's like a spell that they are under.
Trying hard to match his speed
To imitate his every deed,
A noble quest a worthy goal
To reach perfection frees the soul
But few will ever glimpse the heights
Though they may strive with all their might,
Contentment they will have to find
In having known the undersigned.
Sadly, this tale must hold some sorrow

3

For all the firms who hope tomorrow
That he'll appear and work for them
If he doesn't then they'll try again,
To make an offer he can't refuse
So anxious are they all to use
His flawless skills, his experience,
They know they're talking more than pence
To tempt him to fit out their shops
They'll have to pay if they want the tops.

Ode to the Laird

I've worked with fixers from near and far
Some came by train and some by car
Some were thin, some were fat,
Some had white skin and some had black.

Some were good, some were bad,
Some were happy and some were sad,
Some had the crack, some took some flack.
Now as I sit and I look back.

I try to keep my mind on track,
Mulling over this and that
Assisted by the noble vine;
I've heard it said there's truth in wine.

I try to think who was the best,
Which one stood out from all the rest,
There is no doubt, I must insist
His nibs the Laird, he tops the list.

The Dilemma of Horace Plod

Standing firm and resolute
Meat cob in hand with mind astute,
Wondering did he need his job,
More than he did his corned beef cob.

The beef cob won, so off he went
Trundling down the road back bent,
Pushing his tool box with mind content
At a decision made, a day well spent.

The Laird
(High Commissioner)

I've seen the Laird at work and play
I've even seen him making hay,
A photograph as proof have I
You know the camera doesn't lie.

And now commissioner is he
With fisheries to oversee,
Another honour bestowed by men
Upon the Laird of whom they ken.

To this position he will bring
Integrity and all such things,
Befitting one of noble birth
One much revered upon this earth.

Appreciation

For your help and support I think that there ought
To be an award, even make you a Lord,
I know that you'll call it doing your job
But that won't do Jack that's only a fob.

That's how you'll see it and insist it must be
But whatever you say Jack it won't do for me.
Your loyalty, fairness and honest endeavour
Are virtues seen rarely, if indeed ever.

If you hadn't been there, then neither would I
And I mean what I say so there's no need to sigh.
You supported me Jack when I hadn't a prayer
If asked how did I cope; I say Jack Sulley was there.

Harmony

I've loved you now for a thousand years
Through which we've shed too many tears,
Although rarely were they needed
If one of us had only heeded
Mother nature's common sense,
We could've both dropped our defence.

If we had known we could depend
Enough so we could both transcend,
The barriers we built around us
We could have gained so many hours,
And used them in a better way
To bring us sooner to today.

Now harmony I feel so strong,
Why did we have to wait so long
Were we both too blind to see
What was always meant to be,
Eternal love with room to grow
For you I hope, for me I know.

The Repentant Father

I treated my children oh so wrong
And did so for so very long,
I scolded them when I should not
Although I played with them a lot.

They never knew a patient Dad
Just the one who got so mad
The man who seemed to shout at naught,
Who never listened when he aught.

I often worked away from home
And sometimes didn't even phone,
When I was needed face to face
I was in some other place.

I should've paid more heed I know
And given them more help to grow,
With hindsight now, it's clear to see
I didn't give enough of me.

If I had known what I know now
Perhaps I could have changed somehow.
I'll never know, that time is gone
And what we do is forever done.

Though I fell far short of the perfect Dad
Perhaps I haven't been so bad,
For the love we share will always be
Our hearts entwined eternally.

Blissful Ignorance

The damage we do to our children
Trying to bring them up as we are,
With knowledge we base on our ignorance,
I doubt if they'll ever get far.

We learn and we teach but we don't understand
Because our bliss and our ignorance go hand in hand,
We don't stop to think what our words mean or say
Because tomorrow will come and we can laugh at today.

We pretend that we're clever and know what we're about
Because whatever we say, our children don't doubt,
And when they grow up to become as we were
It won't matter to us, because we won't be there.

But will it I wonder, suppose we were wrong,
When we're looking back was there doubt all along.
Will we then be glad that they followed our way,
Or will we regret that we led them astray.

Will the damage we did to our children
By bringing them up as we were,
Cause remorse and a feeling of failure
And will we wish, that we'd taken more care.

Your Time Will Come

In a different time in a different place
It could be you that wins the race;
Your time will come, perhaps it's been
The day your glory could be seen.

Just because my time is now
There is no need for you to bow,
We're equals in eternity
Just play your part and you will see.

How justice truly will prevail
Don't let it drive you off the rail,
It may be part of some great plan
That does not heed how fast we ran.

My Friend

I met him on a cloudless day
A woeful man in his world of grey,
Haunted by what might have been
The glory sought but never seen.

Wracked by doubt taunted by fate
Mocked by what he left too late,
He isn't where he'd meant to be
He may perhaps be you or me.

To fret is futile, time will see
Fulfilment of his destiny,
A struggle long and hard decrees
The pathway home to perfect peace.

Unfulfilled

His happiness he can't sustain
It always seems to end in pain,
The sorrow shows upon his face
He tries to wear it with good grace.

If only he knew what he wanted
Perhaps he wouldn't look so haunted,
Success he craves just like the rest
A pity that he's not the best.

Enthusiasm not sustained
Has cost him what he might have gained.
If only he'd made up his mind
To concentrate on what he had,
Things might not have been so bad.

Memory Lane

Take a trip
Down memory lane,
Take a trip
Do you feel the pain,
Take a trip
Tell me what did you gain,
Was it worth all that travelling
Down memory lane.

An Absent Daughter

O daughter dear we're over here
And you are over there,
I thought I'd write this little rhyme
To show how much we care.

We love and miss you every day
So please have fun whilst you're away,
If you are happy, we're happy too
It helps us bear not being with you.

Trial by Nile

I went by boat upon the Nile
To take the sun and rest awhile
I met some people just by chance,
I should've spared the second glance.

Before I knew it, I was caught
In company that had I aught,
If I had been more diligent,
To have passed by with my head bent.

There's Peter with his caustic wit
And Eric talks a load of ....
I don't know what to make of Stan
Let alone the fearsome Jan.

There's my wife, 'yes dear,' enough said
And Margaret's look could kill you dead,
If they had all been more like Jean
I would have swum the bloody stream.

The Galloping Grandma

The starting pistol splits the air
The race begins the fans are there,
The runners jockeying about
Trying to push our Granny out,
One lap, two laps, three then four
There's lots of time there's plenty more.

Our heroine is well tucked in
The race is hotting up
The opposition have no chance
She's selling them a pup,
The crowd roars on the local lass
As she pulls out and starts to pass.

The race is on, the tapes in sight
Our Granny stumbles what a fright,
But iron willed she's fighting back
Will nothing make this lady crack,
Arms pumping like a hornet's wings
She breasts the tape, of course she wins.

The Laird at Fifty

The Laird is fifty my oh my
How the grey shows through the dye,
A half a century not out
He's still in charge though, there's no doubt.

Across the hill in autumnal splendour
Deterring any would be pretender,
The forest bears his name with pride
In letters written four miles wide.

The Laird's expanding now in size
Both corporation and business wise,
With handmade sheds and garden seats
Vast tracts of land and flocks of sheep.

Silverware adorns his house
With trophies for bowling and shooting grouse,
His fishing prowess is legendary
With stories told from Cork to Derry.

The empire building goes on and on
The legend grows of the noble one,
In country folklore, his name is praised
I wonder how long 'til a statue is raised.

Love Must Be

Eternity is the blink of an eye
Compared to a love that will never die,
Deepest space a little place
Compared to the depths of loves embrace.

When two hearts equally adore
They span the universe and more,
Through endless time as one combined
Their love is paradise defined.

Hearts that beat in perfect time
Make all the bells in heaven chime,
For throughout creation love's the key,
We all must love and love must be.

Observations and Interpretations

All things exist by virtue of their opposite
If light didn't exist, would we know it was dark.
The value of all things is decreed by their opposite
So, scorn not the meek and praise not the mighty
For if all were mighty then all would be meek.

Feel no pain for your station or for your contribution
For yours is as important as any other,
Your place in the universe, as rightful as all others
All creation asks, using the gifts that we have,
Is that we be the best that we can be.

Old Leaky

Old Leaky was a plumber, a man of no renown
He came to make his fortune in dear old London Town,
His crude attempts to ply his trade, inadequate at best
Showed no finesse or expertise to keep the man abreast.

Old Leaky drove around the town in a big white van
He rode around in circles, without purpose or a plan,
Hoping for a start somewhere, his chances were quite slim
For everywhere that Leaky went it seems they'd heard of him.

He won't say where he came from, his references are false
A shame they might have listed his myriads of faults,
So if you see his big white van driving round your streets
Be sure that you don't let him in, or you'll end up with leaks.

Tara

Mother to all life on earth
Help me be worthy of my birth,
To ease my own and others' pain
Throughout this life and on again;
From rising to the setting sun
Until enlightenment is won,
With help from those who know the way
Guide me, mother, to that day.

Nadir

This wasted life of pain and strife
I've suffered now for years
And all I can remember are
The floods and floods of tears.

When will it end where will I be
Lost in the fog of eternity
What is will be, what will be is
Through all of that to come to this.

Through mental anguish toil and grief
My happiness stolen by an invisible thief
Enveloped in a living hell,
Then condemned forever by my death knell.

No hope no future all is lost
All bridges burned when once they're crossed,
The reaper with his scythe awaits
No endless bliss, no pearly gates.

Despair

Destruction caused by our own offspring
Fractures the pledge of the wedding ring,
Life as we know it rent asunder,
Taste the despair as it pulls you under.

Are we to blame or is it they,
Or a combination that has to pay
The price for being what we are,
The cord will snap if it's stretched too far.

So what then of the consequence
What could we say in our defence,
When all that we once had is lost,
Have we the strength to bear to the cost.

Father to Son

You have to sort your problems out
I'll help you where I can
But in the end, it's down to you,
Now that you're a man.

Don't believe them when they tell you
Things will turn out alright,
For on this planet earth you'll find
There is less day than night.

But amidst the darkness there are times
When the sun shines too,
So cherish them when they appear
They'll help you make it through.

A Fruitless Life

The time will come when we must leave
The maker will our thoughts perceive,
No need to state what's in our hearts
He sees our souls in all their parts.

No need for prayer, too late to care
The time for that was way back where,
If we have another chance
Who knows to what tune we'll dance.

As before we blindly blunder
Casting care and love asunder
To end up where we are today,
No lessons learned, debts still to pay.

Ewen Carruthers
(The man and his music)

Sometimes a poet, even a seer
Often profound, always sincere.
His lyrics though subtle can cut to the core
And just a few words start a craving for more.

Musically gifted his style is unique
In his hands the guitar is empowered to speak,
His voice is melodic and kind to the ear
And the two when combined are a sound to revere.

The intricate blend of music and verse
Crafted with care the subjects diverse,
The quality is constant, the sentiment real
Giving the man and his music a timeless appeal.

Autumn

Autumnal life succeeds to strife
Precedes the winter chill,
The countenance reflects the peace
That now is felt within.

Though pensive the mood
When the future is glimpsed
Of the time that must come
Before we're extinct.

When we always feel cold
And we're always in pain
And even the bold
Succumb to the strain.

But that is the future
And youth is long past,
So indulge in your autumn
Until the last leaf is cast.

Together

These last few months have made me see
That we were always meant to be,
Two hearts entwined, yes yours and mine
Together, like this verse we rhyme.

You are the only one for me
We two as one for all to see,
And even in this world of strife
You will forever, be my life.

Kenny and Me

Immortal though he'll never be
If he'll do for you he'll do for me,
He wasn't much when first we met
And I know I can still improve him yet.

We're fairly pleased with what we've done
But hope that there's still more to come,
Rough edges still to iron out
Like the removal of his need to shout.

But underneath he's not so bad
So long as he gets his pint and his fag,
They keep him sweet and calm him down
And he'll be fine if he doesn't drown.

But time moves on as we know, and how,
Though it's some time since I've seen him now,
We chat on the phone so I know he's OK
And next time we meet Ken, it's your turn to pay.

Love Belongs

If we can live our lives in love
With blessings granted from above,
Then happiness is ours to hold
Joined together by a band of gold.

But if love is just a fleeting thing
That begins to pale when the bells cease to ring,
Then true love I will never see
Please love take flight and leave me be.

If love just comes in fits and starts
Then pass me by for I want no part,
I'd rather not feel loves sweet sting
Better lonely nights than a wedding ring.

But I know a love that's good and true
With strength to always see me through,
A love for all eternity
And I know this love belongs to me.

The Lady of the Sea
(a tribute to Ellen McArthur)

Like some modern Boadicea
A female conqueror of fear,
Aboard Kingfisher heart and soul
You and the boat, two halves of a whole.
Traversing mighty oceans as one
Until together the job is done.
Lessons learned by you and shared with us
Of the human spirits limitlessness,
An inspiration to human kind
How proudly we all follow behind.

Love Confirmed

A year has passed and I know now
That on that day I made my vow,
To love and honour, laugh and cry
To stand beside you 'til I die.

Both heart and head were guiding me
Towards my blessed destiny,
To share my life with the man I love
And count those blessings from above.

So much has happened in that year
That you are my all is crystal clear,
But my greatest joy will ever be,
That you are you and I am me.

George

A loyal friend a single mind
Made George a kind that's hard to find,
Nonconformist heart of gold
Enormous courage both brave and bold,
With forthright views and steadfast nerve
He met life head on and never swerved.
Opinionated some might say
But give me his kind any day;
He stood his ground and was counted out
But by George he gave life a clout.

Resilience

The world all loves a fighter,
Even when they lose
And though you may be hurting now
Your senses badly bruised.

You know it's time to turn the tide
Rebuild your life, restore your pride.
So fix your mind on what you feel,
Then concentrate and make it real.

We may never know the reason why
Things occur that make us cry,
Though times may never be the same
Each step from here is ground you gain.

Remember, hold your head up high
And show the world the reason why
You're proud to be just who you are,
Don't let the past your future mar.

Time the Healer

Life's harder now I'm all alone
Though time is helping to atone,
For there being no one to share
Although many really care.

If time's the answer let it pass
And lead me on to greener grass
Where happiness again prevails
And pain in to the distance pales.

Once more to know the joy of being
My pain and sadness forever fleeing,
Put to flight by life's sweet joy
And passing time the eternal ploy.

Forgive and Forget

Make forgiveness your way
Or we'll have to pay
For the rest of our lives,
How will we survive.

We can't walk through this life
Without trouble and strife,
If mistakes have been made
There's no debt to be paid.

Just forgive and forget
That's the best advice yet,
Tolerate let it go
Or your troubles will grow.

If we harbour a grudge
Imagine we are the judge,
Then we take on a role
That's not ours to hold.

So forgive and forget
That's the best advice yet,
Tolerate let it go
And your spirits will grow.

Yuletide's the Time for Joy

Let the snow reflect your happiness
Good luck to all, good health, God bless,
Enjoy yourselves and take a rest
Yuletide's the time for joy.

When friends and family come around
Have good cheer and take them down
A present from your tree,
Say this one's for you from me.

Then drink the health of one and all
We're so glad that you came to call,
There's Christmas crackers for you to share
And mistletoe for those who dare.

Let the snow reflect your happiness
Good luck to all, good health, God bless,
Enjoy yourselves and take a rest
Yuletide's the time for joy.

False Refuge

Are drugs just an experiment
Or the path on which you're bent,
Dissatisfied with who you are
You drift in space through lands afar.

Your mind embellished with bogus powers,
Induced by drugs you smell the flowers
Of a world existing not in truth,
False refuge of despairing youth.

You cannot cope so hide away
Retreating from a timeless day
You seek a place in which to bide,
Discarding self respect and pride.

Forsaking who you're meant to be
You withdraw from reality
Your senses sinking without trace,
Your life dispersing in disgrace.

You search for hope where there is none,
Quick fixes getting nothing done
Just perpetuation of the same
As each day passes without gain.

And so your world goes round and round,
Or rather it goes up and down
In ever increasing dependency,
Until only death, can set you free.

Futility

Mortgages and consumer goods,
The quest for these and other duds
Prevents the spirits soaring high
And creative souls just wilt and die.

Bogged down by debt, induced by greed
Resulting from a rabid need
To own as much as we can hold,
When analysed it's all fools' gold.

Our demise will eventually,
Emphasise the futility
Of lives spent amassing worldly things,
What use are these when the last bell rings.

Bronze and Gold

Autumn portent of future strife
Harbinger of the end of life
Your glory hides your message well,
Who'd guess the fate your hues foretell.

Bedecked in gold and bronze and green
Your purpose as yet unforeseen,
With stealth, you usher in our doom
By bold pretence of summer's bloom.

Lulled by the splendour of your garb,
Oblivious to the hidden barb
As one by one we wilt and fall,
Discarded leaves the fate of all.

Succeeded then by winters chill,
Designed to break the strongest will
Your work completed by the cold,
Conspirator of bronze and gold.

The Casino

No clocks, no windows, what's the game
Casino man says keep on playing,
You don't need to know the time
Or if or not the sun don't shine.

Shoot some craps, play five card stud
The faro tables looking good,
Try your luck on the slot machine
There's lots to do so don't be mean.

Of time and daylight pay no heed,
My luck will change is the gamblers creed,
Play whilst there's money in your poke
The time to leave is when you're broke.

If now and then you win a hand
It proves we're fair so let it stand,
And when you lose then don't complain
Been nice to meet you, come again.

See You Anon

When I was young and in my prime
I didn't think about the time,
As the days and years flew by
I never even wondered why,
When this day's gone there's plenty more
Who gives a fig for nature's law.

Then suddenly, six decades passed
Who knows which day will be my last,
What is this thing that we call time
What happened to the endless rhyme,
The shock of knowing most is gone
Dare I still say, see you anon?

Did I Peek at Paradise

An angel brushed me with her wings
As she flew gently by
She touched on my emotions
Then left me wondering why.

What purpose did this meeting serve
It caused more pain than joy
But then she knew much more than me
Perhaps that was her ploy.

She let me peek at paradise
Then hid it out of sight
As if she meant to tell me
It was not mine by right.

But how to earn the right to find
What I had briefly seen
Was not it seems for me to know,
Could it have been a dream.

Through years of aimless drifting,
Though this may not be so,
I still don't know where I should look
To find what I should know.

For though she showed me what was there
She did not point the way
But left me there to flounder
Day after endless day.

Now as the end for me draws near
And still with naught to show,
It seems I'll live the whole of life
And still not ever know.

A Cautionary Tale

An airport's not the place to be
For harmless codgers such as me,
Where security and police patrol
Intent on catching some poor soul.

Striving hard to show their might
You bet they have you in their sights,
The slightest misdemeanour will
Their countenance with pleasure fill.

I show my pass to the man at the desk,
Then through the scanner, another test,
Now I'm frisked my pockets searched
What have they found, they've begun to smirk.

And then my spirits really sank
As they report me through the ranks,
From checker up to supervisor
Constable, sergeant, God how much higher.

Looking stern, they read my rights
So many there's no chance of flight,
A caution they think will suffice,
My heinous crime; a pocketknife.

The Ballad of Tommy Ronan

He wasn't big, he wasn't mean,
His way of living was kinda clean,
He drank a bit but he didn't smoke
Tommy Ronan was that kinda bloke.

If he spotted trouble, then he'd skirt around
He'd just slip by without a sound,
He had no truck with the lower kind
But when the chips were down he knew his mind.

It was a day in May when the sun beat down
That Tommy decided he'd ride into town,
As he hitched his horse to the hitching rail
He heard a cry, well more of a wail.

A bunch of guys were picking on a crippled lad
It was this kind of thing that made Tommy mad,
For the one thing that he couldn't stand
Was injustice, so he took a hand.

Tommy called them out and they made their play
But this wasn't going to be their day.
His draw was swift and his aim was good,
It was a coward from behind who spilled Tommy's blood.

The script was written for that fateful day
And Tommy played the part he had to play.
But as he lay dying in the noon day sun,
The crippled boy's tears fell on Tommy's gun.

The Ballad of Tommy Ronan
Part Two

Tommy didn't die from that bullet wound
And the coward knew he'd come looking soon,
The crippled lad had saved Tommy's life
When he dug out the bullet with his pocketknife.

It took some time for the wound to heal
And through his suffering Tommy showed his steel,
The stuff from which men like Tom are made
Is as hard as flint and as cool as jade.

The coward knew that time was getting tight
And he hadn't the stomach for a stand-up fight,
He decided to ride to Tommy's ranch
While Tom was laid up, he was in with a chance.

He got there on a pitch-dark night
Keeping to the shadows and well out of sight,
He sneaked in through an unbarred door
And shook with fear as he crossed the bare board floor.

The crippled boy heard a floorboard creak
As he sat with Tom who was still quite weak,
But since that fateful day in May
Tommy's gun was never far away.

As the coward's gun blazed round the bedroom door
Tommy's gun barked once; the coward was no more.
The debt was paid, the killing done
And the crippled boy holstered Tommy's gun.

A Bygone Age

Paper boys and postmen scurrying around
Milkmen with bottles clinking carrying on their rounds,
The sounds of morning long ago
Awakening the world to sunshine or snow.

Then later on the coalman black
With sacks of coal upon his back
Grunting and sweating under the strain,
Out in all weathers sunshine or rain.

These were the tradesmen of a bygone age
The world was then a different stage,
No internet, nor world wide web
Just honest toil for their daily bread.

La Différence

In a world that wore a different face
Where masculinity had its place,
Housework was done by comely wives
Whilst men supported both their lives.

As time goes by if the roles reverse
Will it be better or will it be worse,
Would it not cause a major glitch
And could we cope with such a switch.

How will we know who we are then
What will determine women from men,
If we were one, we'd never know
The joys la différence could bestow.

So think about it one more time
Before you cast aside this rhyme,
This joyous state if not retained
Perchance may never be regained.

Life Begins...

Forty is a woman's stage
The day she truly comes of age,
Still youthful yet mature and wise
With mystery lurking in her eyes.

The life she's lived until this day
Has taught her how to hold her sway,
With poise and dignity to spare
Her countenance says, treat with care.

Desirable yet - and still a prize
She captivates in any guise
Her woman's wiles perfected now,
A girl no more, she takes her bow.

A Hint of Nectar

The last of our summer wine
A vintage that was so sublime,
The harvest of the sweetest vine
Proclaimed our summer time.

But now that those days are gone
Our time is done, we must move on,
Vacate this space for those behind
To taste the fruit of all they find.

As all good things must surely end
There's no more turns and no more bends,
There's just one road it's straight ahead
Our earthly loads can now be shed.

Leave all your cares and woes behind
Together with your summer time,
For destiny where e'er it be
May deviate twixt you and me.

Just one last sip of summer wine
Selected from the sweetest vine,
A hint of nectar so divine,
Our final taste of summer time.

Antarctica

Endless waste of snow and ice
Howling wind and deep crevasse,
Mariners hunting pods of whales
Albatross braving winter gales.

Orca hunting seals in packs,
Penguins trying to make it back
To the safety of the beach
Way beyond the killers' reach.

Forests of kelp, clouds of krill
Their fate the mighty whales to fill,
Gigantic icebergs and mountainous seas;
Antarctica is all of these.

Veils of Tears

You've left us now you've gone for good
It hurts like hell I knew it would,
The loss no less for all your years
Bereaved we mourn through veils of tears.

Now never more to see your face
Nor feel the warmth of your embrace,
Our world diminished by your demise
The focal point gone from our lives.

You nurtured me and helped me grow
And when the tears no longer flow,
With gratitude your life I'll see
I know you did your best for me.

But as for now, despair I know
With no more chance my love to show,
Cruel fate decreed it was your time
Now all I have is in my mind.

And in my mind you'll ever be,
Far more than just a memory
For what can never be undone,
Is that undying love of a mother's son.

Granny's Aconites

January brings your Aconites
Like brightly shining yellow lights
Nestling in their beds of green
Demanding boldly to be seen.

Through February they reign supreme,
With all around still in a dream
And winters chill still in the ground
They tell of spring but make no sound.

In March they disappear from view
But they will bloom again for you
And as your light shines ever bright,
Each year so will your Aconites.

Retirement

Meet some people have a chat
About nothing much, just this and that.
Wander aimlessly around
On the bus and in to town,
Getting under peoples' feet
As I meander around the streets.

Finances flowing out not in
'Til nothings left; not if but when,
Aches and pains increase with time
And life no longer seems to rhyme,
The future shorter now, more bleak
Dissipating week by week.

Sitting back, we watch it pass
Not knowing how long it will last,
So aimlessly we carry on
Just waiting 'til our days are done.
Our passing mourned by some we knew;
We disappear from earthly view.

Nature's Way

Transmutation taking place
At natures unrelenting pace,
No hesitation in her quest
Adapting all to her behest,
The world continually shaped and changed,
There's nothing new; just rearranged.

The Languid Pool

This languid, deep, mysterious pool
Tranquil epitome of cool,
Can change from calm benignity
In to a wild pulsating sea.

Brave are those who venture near
This raging tempest without fear,
The primal forces when enraged
Leaves no escape if once engaged.

Waves of unrestrained desire
Surging, breaking ever higher,
With fervid passions unabated
Until entirely satiated.

The Wooden Church
(Honfleur)

O wondrous wooden house of God
With modest shingles though you're clad
Your beauty lies within the eye
Of those who chance to pass you by.
Dutch by design though built in France;
Was it meant or circumstance,
Be the reasons as they may
The faithful have their place to pray.

Isolation

Words of love unspoken yet again
Another night of loneliness and pain,
No tender hugs nor yet a warm caress
No union to show that they are blessed.

Yet on each other they depend
The habit easy to defend,
With grudges comforting to nurse
To live alone could be far worse.

So they continue to pretend
Through waking hours till dusk descends,
Then darkness brings with days' cessation
Tormented nights of isolation.

Playtime at Grandad's
(And don't forget Lolly)

When you were just a little tot
You always liked to play a lot,
Think of a game Grandad you'd cry
Then expect it done in the blink of an eye.

We'd play at chase and hide and seek
You'd hide so well not even a squeak,
In the cupboard behind the chair
In the linen basket with no room to spare.

Best not to mention my great big blue nappy
That you had to change when I'd filled it with 'pappy',
Then came the injections and those damned safety pins
The nurse's outfit you just happened to bring.

And what about Nellie my ginormous girlfriend
The things she would do in our games of 'betend',
World War Two with Nana the siren
That sounded as if she'd swallowed her iron.

Queuing at the bank across the kitchen and back
Arrive at the counter as you'd run out of cash,
Then Nellie again coming down to your gym
But because of her size she couldn't get in.

And then what about 'Cluella the Ville'
Locked up in jail but escaping at will,
To steal your Dalmatians once again 'Oh!' my golly'
I can't write this rhyme without mentioning Lolly.

From when you awoke and for the rest of the day
Your only concern was to make Grandad play,
Our days would be full of laughter and joy
Your Daddy once said I was your favourite toy.

The biff on the button phew that was a pain
Since that fateful day I've not been the same,
And now you are grown, and those days are gone
But Katie the memories will live on and on.

The Ageing Laird

The Lairds nearing now three score and ten
But those who knew him way back when,
Will recognise the style and skill
Applied more slowly now but still
Performed with accuracy and care
If not with former speed and flair.
Though ageing gracefully, we ken
He's nearing now three score and ten.

Ireland's Little Men

I wrote a song of Ireland
I wrote it in me sleep,
For Ireland is a land of dreams
And dreams we all can keep.
In troubled times when far from home
My dreams belong to me
And though I'll let you share my dream
It's best you go and see.

I wrote a song of Ireland
I wrote it with me pen,
I wrote it once, I wrote it twice,
I wrote it once again.
I wrote it down in reverence
Of Ireland's little men.

So if you visit Ireland,
It makes no matter when
And happen on a fairy ring
In some enchanted glen;
Don't enter there and be aware
Of those you will not see
Then hurry on your journey
And leave things as they be.
For Ireland is a land of dreams,
So don't take chances when
You may be in the company
Of Ireland's little men.

I wrote a song of Ireland
I wrote it with me pen,
I wrote it once, I wrote it twice,
I wrote it once again.
But I wrote it more in reverence
Of Ireland's little men.

I For-to-got

We met on the day that you were born
Your story began in the early morn,
You wouldn't be still for more than a mo'
From morning 'til night you were on the go.

When you heard music you'd be on the move
From the day you were born you slipped in to the groove,
Wriggling about in time to the beat
Long before you could stand on your feet.

When you slept in the day it was a half hour crash
Then no coming round, you awoke in a flash,
With your bright blue eyes and your blonde blonde hair
You were designed to cause a bit of a stir.

Then as you grew and started to speak
And you went to nursery week by week,
It wasn't long before you knew
How to tell Grandad what to do.

When playing nurseries in your home
In and out from room to room,
'I'm back,' you'd say as you came through the door
When you hadn't been gone for 'one mimit' or more.

Some more of your sayings I've listed here
So we can keep your childhood near
Are 'nims and peedles' and 'I for-to-got'
There seems to be an awful lot.

'I've got sunny eyes' when the suns in your eyes
And 'how many corners' when out for a drive,
You doubled your words instead of just one
Like 'really really,' and 'what did you say' instead of pardon.

You'd always say hello in the street
To everyone that you happened to meet,
With 'what's your name' and 'where've you been,'
'How old are you;' at this they'd beam.

Then later on as you started to grow
You'd say, 'I'm in the middle' when you didn't quite know.
There's so much more, I could go on for 'ever ever'
But suffice to say Emmy May, you're a blether.

Shut up Grandad!

Two Granddaughters and then a boy
We thought how marvellous, what a joy,
And so it was for just a year
Then your assault began upon the ear.

You twiddled your hair and sucked your thumb
Then all of a sudden everything was a drum,
You bashed everything that you could reach
And ate all the sand you could find on the beach.

Talking of eating, now that's serious stuff
When it came to food there was never enough,
Any hope of a share in a sausage was out
And the chance of a blueberry, always in doubt.

The 'barjecue' was your favourite thing
Though it was in the shower you started sing,
'Square' words you knew that their use you would rue,
But fibbing you thought it was OK to do.

You love riding your bike and as you peddle away
You say 'shut up Grandad' but it's only in play,
You play air guitar in front of the telly
And when I play my piano, you shake like a jelly.

When we play, you want me to walk like a duck
Because then I'm so slow and I can't catch you up,
You tease from afar and know that you're safe
Then you laugh so much that you cannot escape.

Dandan my little man you're a star when you're good
And a great little helper when I'm working with wood,
You helped pull down the tree in your garden that day,
And you chattered so much that there's no more to say.

The Inside Forward
Inspired by Tommy Asher

Short and sturdy, hard as nails
Tireless legs that never failed,
He held his own against the best
And in his wake, he left the rest.

A career that started out so bright
Was not to reach the promised heights,
Not for want of talent though
The big rewards he would forego.

Those who knew the game would say
There was no doubt the lad could play,
The fire inside that drove him on
Was checked by those who deal and con.

Who can say what might have been
If he had graced the bigger scene,
He had the skill, he had the verve
And none could say he lacked the nerve.

Since from the game he took his bow
His life's moved on, his passion now,
His grandkids playing on the floor
And Tommy would not ask for more.

Not Beyond Midnight

When Midnight comes it's time to go
The hour when I must end the show,
It's no reflection on your skill
Nor if your role you did fulfil.

The day is done, as it has to be
The book must close on you and me,
To carry on would not be right
So we must part in dead of night.

No argument can change my mind
As midnight seeks two days to bind,
And I must leave before that hour
Lest I fall victim to your power.

It's no fault of your tender love
But I am bound to one above,
One who was but is no more
One I still yearn for and adore.

The Gardener

Dressed in black amongst the green
Allows the gardener to be seen,
Though unobtrusive he is there
Tending all within his care.

Patience is his stock in trade
Whilst directing mowers blade,
Pruning, trimming, planting out
Undeterred by flood or drought.

The garden then in turn displays
In harmony with nature's ways,
The glory of each seasons splendour
The man in black works on in wonder.

The Fugitive

Hidden from me for all these years
Knowledge of myself is in arrears,
Who is he that I call me
Do I want to know what I may be?

Better that I'm hidden from view
That knowledge best left to the few,
More fit to cope with truth and clarity
Without risk to me of despair or vanity.

But how long can I hide myself
How long do I sit on the shelf,
Hoping that I'll never see
Nor have to face, he that is me.

Then and Now

You pose in your designer wear
Pushing buttons everywhere,
The world deskilled the tradesmen dead
Care and pride both put to bed.

You never felt the furnace blast
Were never called upon to cast,
All of that is dead and gone
Life as they say has now moved on.

So read this rhyme it won't take long
Then decide yourself if it's right or wrong,
The nature of the work has changed
But nothing else is rearranged.

From pit face to computer screen
The working class have ever been,
Victims of their boss's greed
Forced to fight and then concede.

Robbed of their dues by those on high
Who, once elected their vows belie,
Whilst the banks' behaviour, mean and crass
Confirms the fate of the working class.

Sam

We felt love like we'd never known
Right from the day that you were born,
Which made almost too much to bear
Your struggle through intensive care.

To see you there our precious son
Almost left our lives undone,
And anxious though we were for you
Sam, you were tougher than we knew.

Together with the medic's skill
And your indomitable will,
All the setbacks you defied
Your courage would not be denied.

You persevered Sam bit by bit
Now one year on and fighting fit,
Our lives you fill with endless joy
Our very special little boy.

Bear with Me

Don't judge me by what I am now
Nor be concerned with why or how,
Whatever life's demands decree
We all must face our destiny.

I did not choose what I've become
This curse to which I now succumb,
Has robbed me of my life's control
Afflicting body, heart and soul.

Bereft of senses, hope and pride
The me you knew, now cast aside,
My life now sadly in decline
As I withdraw in to my mind.

Bear with me, tolerate my plight
Stand by me as I lose this fight,
And if or when you think of me
Remember who I used to be.

John

Your life cut short, for us it's true
But there was nothing we could do,
You won't grow old nor fall apart
Not frail, nor ill, you've played your part.

The fifty happy years you knew
We're so glad that we shared with you,
We mourn our loss; we'll miss you John
And the joy you brought to everyone.

With your love of life for all to see
Our memories will always be,
Of one whose friendship was the best
John those you knew were truly blessed.

Ireland

The mysticism of the land
From mountain top to beaches' sand,
From woodland to the lonely moor
And all around her rocky shore.

The wisdom in her ballads' lines
Rooted in her ancient rhymes,
Penned by poets of varied hue
Insightful, yet mysterious too.

All of this is Ireland
Where truth and myth go hand in hand,
The blend is seamless but to few
Who know the secrets hidden from view.

So harken to the fairy tale
That stems from way beyond the pale,
Where myth and legend both arise
And truth is seen through knowing eyes.

Knowing does not come with age,
As likely, is the youthful sage,
Though rare are those empowered to see,
What has been and what will be.

John
The Send Off

People streaming through the door
The place is full, yet there are more
Crammed into the vestibule,
Where standing only is the rule.

They can't have known him surely not,
Not all of them, there's such a lot
But each one has a tale to tell;
It seems they knew him very well.

He spent his life amassing friends
A list so long it never ends,
Cricketers, golfers, football fans
It was like the gathering of the clans.

Workmates too, more than a few
All thinking crikey! What a do,
Socialites and movie stars
Wouldn't fill as many cars.

John didn't need their wealth or fame
With friends too numerous to name,
And though, if somewhat unrefined
He was indeed one of a kind.

The Bully

The wheels of fate have turned your way
But I still have my debts to pay,
What I am now is nothing more,
My self-esteem still on the floor.

I'm glad the pain and hurt have gone
That you grew strong, kept moving on,
Remorse alas won't set me free,
I am where I deserve to be.

I was the bully, the empty shell
The one who made your school days' hell,
The empty shell, the nowhere man
The one who'd say 'because I can'.

Forgiveness I do not desire
I do not seek to quell your ire,
This burden I must always bear,
Lest henceforth I forget to care.

Choirboys
All Saints, Turnditch

Choirboys we were back then
When the choirs' best were Colin and Ken,
Pumping the organ, we saw as a chore
A job we all thought was a bit of a bore.

Tolling the bell was also a task
For a methodical 'dong' the Vicar would ask,
A 'ding-dong' was frowned on and if ever heard,
Brought wrathful rebuke from our man of the word.

Mrs Wagstaff played organ and she was a gem
But his Reverence the Vicar well he was, ahem!
The old boy liked to think that the church was the hub,
But when the service was done we adjourned to the pub.

Where we'd all sing the praises of old Harry R.
With much more gusto than when in the choir,
A landlord of note and a worthy old gent,
Brown ale in 'The Tiger' was money well spent.

The Space Between

The space between them wider now
Gives cause to ponder why and how,
They once seemed close, alas in vain
Their passion brief, now on the wane.

It's hard to know just how they feel
Or if or not the breach can heal,
Options many been and gone
Yet they still choose to carry on.

To live a life devoid of rhyme
Seems a gross abuse of time,
Existing only day by day
Till life itself has ebbed away.

So sad if this should be their fate
Brought on by what they left too late,
There'll be no second chance it seems
Should they pursue conflicting dreams.

The Poet's Pain

Whilst all around him dream and sleep
The poet lies awake and weeps,
His tears are shed for things unknown
To those of more prosaic tone.

He writes of things that he has seen
In places, only he has been,
Awareness varies day by day
Sometimes clear and sometimes grey.

Perception veering from the norm
And melancholy so forlorn,
Brings about the written verse
His talent also is his curse.

He lives his life upon the edge
Precarious, on a narrow ledge,
Nerves stretched taut he strives to see
What has been and what will be.

The text compiled with good intent
Concerning life and its laments,
In language he can understand
With words he has at his command.

Once written, his perceptions change
His thoughts unbidden rearrange,
The verse that once expressed his view
Is now just what it means to you.

The Wedding

A splendid time was had by all
At the happy couple's wedding ball,
The ladies were a sight to see
Resplendent in their finery.

Bridesmaids attired in stylish dresses
Enhanced by elegant coiffured tresses,
The groom, best man and ushers to
'Steady girls; just form a queue'.

All thinking that they looked just so,
Until the page boy stole the show,
In classic tails and shiny shoes,
The ladies were all his to choose.

The parents of the bride and groom
No longer young but still in bloom,
With dignified and cultured mien
Compliments the wedding scene.

And then the bride in grand array
Arrives in style to claim her day,
Her countenance, her poise, her grace
Announced to all her rightful place.

Life in a Derbyshire Village
Boyhood Memories – 1950's

Through the woods and o'er the leas,
Kicking a ball or climbing trees
Along the valley by the brook
catching fish without a hook.

The brook in which we learned to swim
Scrambling out to jump back in,
About our strokes we could not gloat
In spite of which we stayed afloat.

Dawdling back; we had all day,
Skimming stones along the way,
Through the ford if not in flood
Then by New Road; to Ireton Wood.

An arduous climb up Cat Hall Lane
With fruit to scrump to ease the pain,
Via Cross O'Th Hands then all downhill
Tomorrow there'd by fields to till.

To cope with seasonal demand
We'd help the farmers work the land,
From drilling seed as hedgerows bud;
To picking spuds in the cold and mud.

Leading hay with horse and dray
Long hours of work for meagre pay,
Though true to say and fair to tell,
At threshing time, they fed us well.

When not engaged for little gain
Football was the favoured game,
Till twilight fell we played all day
Then to 'The Tiger' we would stray.

There were no street lights then of course
Our favourite pub our last recourse,
Enabled by an outside light
The game went on into the night.

A floodlit pitch was hard to find
Way back in nineteen fifty-nine,
Which made us luckier than most
With one provided by 'mine host'.

We'd venture in before too long
A drink of something, not too strong,
Not at first, though this would change
As our desires would rearrange.

On Thursday evenings, we'd a date
Choir practice, don't be late,
Always late though getting away
Encroaching on our time to play.

Until a boy I will not name
Concluded we'd ourselves to blame,
So he dreamed up a cunning ploy
To dent our Pastor's choral joy.

An alarm clock underneath his coat
Caught the cleric out mid-note,
You can well imagine our leader's ire
As he blew his top at all the choir.

The perpetrator acting alone
Had no effect on the Vicar's tone,
All were guilty in his view
But then alas, what could he do.

His role relied on our goodwill
Without it he'd no choir to drill,
So to prove he could he kept us late
Then stomped off out the churchyard gate.

As suitably admonished we,
Repaired to where we liked to be,
We knew the way, no need to fuss
An outside light was guiding us.

We hurried on, it wasn't far
With a tale to tell in our local bar,
And a well-earned pint, or maybe two
You can bet the Reverend had a few.

Another time that I recall
Of a local Vicar taking a fall,
When he was clouted up the rear
By a cyclist riding in top gear.

Severely shaken by the blow
The cleric kept his profile low,
To hide a bump as red as a rose
Where else but on his 'Parson's nose'.

On the cyclists name we will not dwell
And the Priest survived, so all was well,
Whilst these tales recalled through mists of time
Are now immortalised in rhyme.

The Lost Child

A child lost in the fog of life,
Is a child born to a world of strife,
For him, life will be always hard
His hand dealt with a bogus card.

Light-hearted though he seems to be
He thinks more deeply than we see,
The joys of living he will not reap
His respite only when at sleep.

Always outside looking in
His rightful place eluding him,
With inmost thoughts he cannot share
He fits in neither here nor there.

This child resides within us all,
In some alas there's nothing more,
His life it seems will always be
Bedevilled by anxiety.

Muhammad Ali

I regret I couldn't write this whilst you were still alive
Muhammad please believe me, I tried and tried and tried,
But now you're gone it seems as if my pen just won't be still
Your passing hard to swallow, is such a bitter pill.

It's like I really knew you, you were the centre of the world
You meant something to everyone because you really cared,
The word's still full of all the things that you once said and did
Your bravery in adversity, the fact you never hid.

Not even from Great Uncle Sam, you took him on and won
I remember well the time that you, refused to shoot his gun
He robbed you of your greatest years, when you refused the draft
Your resolute audacity left all the world aghast.

Your boxing gave you glory but you were a bigger man than that
You taught important lessons with the wisdom in your chat,
The way you lived your troubled life throughout your mortal coil
Is a lesson for us all to learn, no matter how we toil.

Frank Morley

In a chapel crypt, it all began
Submission wrestling was the plan,
The rules as such were vague and few
There wasn't much you couldn't do.

You couldn't kick or gouge or bite
Unless you did it out of sight,
And, if someone broke a limb
That was entirely up to him.

Submit or suffer was the rule
Show was meant for playing the fool,
With Mauler Morley, Barry Kaye
And Golden Boy all holding sway.

Then came freestyle, a different game
At first it all seemed rather tame,
With a ref' and judges keeping score
Points and pinfalls, rules galore.

Despite all this it could be rough
With competition fierce and tough,
A truth impossible to deny
As cauliflower ears will testify.

The first generation did OK
Inspired by Frank they paved the way,
For others who would follow on
With victories and titles won.

And as for Frank, he in his turn
Had different coaching skills to learn,
He relished the task and saw it through
Setting the goals, they'd then pursue.

His dedication, drive and vision
Allowed no room for indecision,
Whilst his motivation, well ingrained
Was clearly seen in those he trained.

So wrestlers all, both old and new
Should have no doubt that Frank is due,
Their everlasting gratitude
Regardless of their aptitude.

Casualties

Casualties of government, we're all part of their game,
No longer individual's, we're treated all the same
A commodity to our employers, a number on a card
A statistic to our leaders who show us scant regard.

Our politicians treat us like we're stupid clods of earth
And in between elections, seek to denigrate our worth,
Unless they want to pass the buck, they like to ask us then
So someone else can take the blame; it won't be down to them.

Our schools obsessed with SATs results are just about the same,
Much more concerned with Ofsted than intellectual gain
The teachers with their inset days; have they the time to spare,
Seem less concerned with teaching than their egocentric care.

I don't believe the Health Service doesn't care at all
But inefficient admin, has it backed against the wall,
My childhood doctor was on call, each and every day
He had no need of management, to organise his way.

Nor did he have the luxury of browsing on a screen
But always found the time to see who needed to be seen,
To do his rounds he had a bike or rode a borrowed horse
Nowadays they work part time, with a Mercedes car of course.

The apathetic point of view will reap what it deserves
We can of course, if we so wish, reverse this downward curve,
If we sit back and ring our hands, events will grind us down
We either choose to stand and fight or wallow 'til we drown.

For now, that's all I have to say, I've had my little moan
I don't believe these viewpoints though, are only mine alone
But there it is, it's how I feel, so take it as you will
Form your opinions for yourself and swallow your own pill.

Nature's Sounds

Harkening to all around
Listening in to nature's sounds,
A skylark singing high above
The cooing of an amorous dove.

A blackbird calling from a bush
The tuneful renderings of the thrush,
A barn owl screeching leaves the byre
All part of nature's wondrous choir.

The lapwing feigns an injured wing
As she creates a gambler's sting,
Deceived, the predator gives chase
At which she launches in to space.

Peewit she calls from way on high
Mocking the hunter from the sky,
Whilst circling round, her nest in view
Scanning the land for dangers new.

Within the confines of our bounds
Our attention turns towards the ground,
Strange noises from the undergrowth
Confirming life or death, or both.

Small creatures scurrying out of sight
To places where there is no light,
Scuffling, grunting, sounds of strife
The unrelenting fight for life.